DinoZone

MEAT-EATING DINOSAURS

KATIE WOOLLEY

WINDMILL
BOOKS

Published in 2017 by **Windmill Books**, an Imprint of Rosen Publishing
29 East 21st Street, New York, NY 10010

Author: Katie Woolley
Designers: Neal Cobourne and Emma Randall
Editors: Joe Harris and Anna Brett

Picture credits: Cover illustration: Rudolf Farkas. Interior illustrations: Arcturus Image Library (Stefano Azzalin: 5, 14, 18, 22l, 23l, 27; Martin Bustamante: 7, 12, 13, 16, 19, 20; Juan Calle: 10, 11, 15, 17, 21, 22r; Liberum Donum: 25; Colin Howard: 26; Kunal Kundu: 9; Val Walerczuk: 4); and Shutterstock: 7, 29 (Key: b-bottom, t-top, c-center, l-left, r-right).

Cataloging-in-Publication Data
Names: Woolley, Katie.
Title: Meat-eating dinosaurs / Katie Woolley.
Description: New York : Windmill Books, 2017. | Series: Dinozone | Includes index.
Identifiers: ISBN 9781499481662 (pbk.) | ISBN 9781499481679 (library bound) |
  ISBN 9781508192855 (6 pack)
Subjects: LCSH: Dinosaurs--Juvenile literature. | Carnivorous animals, Fossil--Juvenile literature.
Classification: LCC QE861.5 W66 2017 | DDC 567.9--dc23

Manufactured in the United States of America
CPSIA Compliance Information: Batch #BW17PK: For Further Information contact Rosen Publishing, New York, New York at 1-800-237-9932

CONTENTS

Mighty meat eaters

Meat-eating dinosaurs—the carnivores—were fast-moving, deadly hunters. They had razor-sharp teeth, strong back legs, and hooked claws on the ends of their toes.

Meat-eating dinosaurs lived throughout the Triassic, Jurassic, and Cretaceous periods. *Allosaurus* (AH-loh-SORE-us) lived during the Jurassic period.

Allosaurus

Long tail to balance out neck and head

Big, sharp teeth

Short arms

Claws

Long, strong back legs

Acrocanthosaurus (ah-crow-CAN-thoh-SORE-us) was a meat eater with spines growing out of its back. It lived during the early Cretaceous period.

Most theropods walked on two legs. Theropod means **"beast–footed."**

Fast Facts

Most meat-eating dinosaurs were theropods (THEH-roh-pods). Some, such as *Allosaurus* and *Acrocanthosaurus*, were huge. Others were tiny.

Acrocanthosaurus

Sharp teeth

Fossilized teeth can help us learn more about dinosaurs. The teeth of a *Tyrannosaurus rex* (tie-RAN-oh-SORE-us REX) were about 9 inches (23 cm) long. That's as long as a banana!

Some meat-eating dinosaurs were hunters, while some were scavengers, like modern hyenas. *T. rex* may have been both!

The first dinosaurs were carnivores. Plant eaters arrived later!

Meat-eating dinosaurs' powerful jaws snapped shut like a crocodile's. Their pointed teeth could pierce flesh and crush bones of bigger prey, such as *Stegosaurus* (STEH-goh-SORE-us). Some meat eaters had serrated (saw-like) teeth that could rip off chunks of flesh and bone as they ate.

A theropod skull

A theropod feasting on its prey.

The thorny lizard

The largest meat-eating dinosaur was *Spinosaurus* (SPINE-oh-SORE-us). It was the length of two buses. The spines on its back were covered in skin, and looked like a sail. Each spine measured up to 6.5 feet (2 m) high—that's taller than most adults!

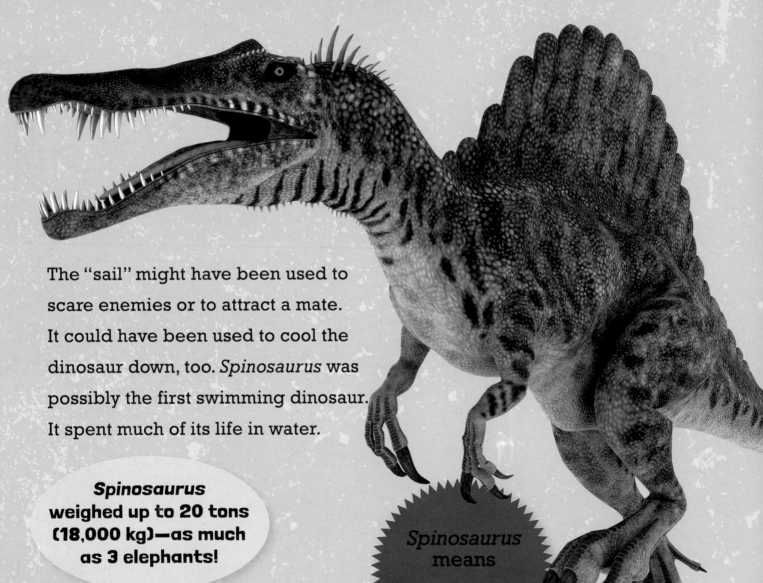

The "sail" might have been used to scare enemies or to attract a mate. It could have been used to cool the dinosaur down, too. *Spinosaurus* was possibly the first swimming dinosaur. It spent much of its life in water.

Spinosaurus weighed up to 20 tons (18,000 kg)—as much as 3 elephants!

Spinosaurus means "thorn lizard."

Fast Facts

When: Late Cretaceous period

Food: Other dinosaurs and large fish

Size: 59 feet (18 m) long

You!

Weight: 4.4 tons (4,000 kg)

How it moved: On two legs

Found in: Egypt and Morocco, Africa

Spinosaurus lived during the Cretaceous period, roaming the swamps of North Africa. It may have eaten dinosaurs, such as sauropods, as well as sharks and other large fish.

A tiny hunter

Hesperonychus (hes-puh-ruh-NIE-kus) was one of the smallest meat-eating dinosaurs that ever lived in North America. It was about the size of a pet cat. It was a deadly predator, although its prey was much smaller than *T. rex's*!

This tiny meat eater ran on two legs and had an enlarged claw on its second toe. It probably hunted for food such as insects and small mammals. Forests and marshes were its hunting grounds.

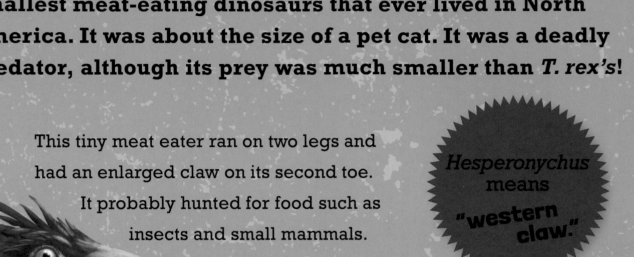

Hesperonychus means **"western claw."**

Fast Facts

When: Late Cretaceous period

Food: Probably insects and small mammals

Size: 24 in (60 cm) long

You!

Weight: 4 lb (1.9 kg)

How it moved: On two legs

Found in: North America

Hesperonychus weighed about as much as a chicken.

Hesperonychus may have had feathered wings that helped it glide from tree to tree. This way, it avoided larger predators on the ground.

Lone hunters or pack killers?

Some meat-eating dinosaurs hunted on their own, like tigers and bears. Others hunted in a pack, like wolves. We know this from fossils that show them living alone or in groups.

Yangchuanosaurus (yang-choo-AN-oh-SORE-us) was 33 feet (10 m) long—that's the length of two cars. But it may still have stalked its prey in packs.

Mamenchisaurus

Yangchuanosaurus

Pack hunting would have made it easier to overcome larger prey, such as *Mamenchisaurus* (MAH-men-kee-SORE-us).

Fast Facts

Some meat eaters may have had saliva full of deadly bacteria. One bite could have poisoned and killed a victim!

Eoraptor (EE-oh-rap-tor) was one of the earliest pack hunters. It had large eyes to see prey from far away.

Eoraptors

Fish for supper?

Suchomimus (SOO-koh-MIM-us) was a large dinosaur with a body that was adapted for eating fish. Its long snout and huge claws were perfect for catching its slippery prey.

Suchomimus

Fast Facts

When: Early Cretaceous period

Food: Fish

Size: 33 ft (10 m) long

You!

Weight: 2.2 tons (2,000 kg)

How it moved: On two legs

Found in: United Kingdom and Spain, Europe

Baryonyx (bah-ree-ON-icks) was a fish-eating dinosaur with a jaw like a crocodile's. It probably waded in water, waiting for its supper to swim by. Then it would use its large thumb claw like a hook, to stab a passing fish.

Baryonyx's teeth had a jagged edge, like a saw. They were curved inward, making it very hard for a fish to escape!

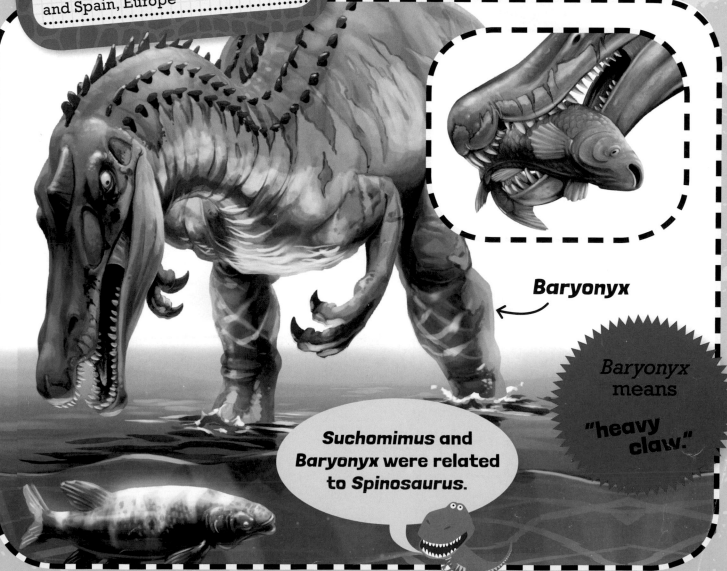

Baryonyx

Baryonyx means **"heavy claw."**

Suchomimus and Baryonyx were related to Spinosaurus.

Small but deadly

Aggressive, light, small, and speedy, *Velociraptor* (veh-LAH-suh-rap-tor) was a ferocious predator. It was armed with sharp teeth and claws like daggers. A pack of these hunters could easily catch its prey.

Fast Facts

When: Late Cretaceous period

Food: Other animals

Size: 6 ft (1.8 m) long

← You!

Weight: 15-33 lb (7-15 kg)

How it moved: On two legs

Found in: Mongolia, Asia

Velociraptor was the size of a large dog and had strong back legs. It could run at up to 40 miles (64 km) per hour. This meat eater had 80 teeth and arms with three-fingered claws. A fearsome sight!

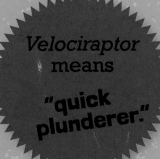

Velociraptor means "quick plunderer."

Velociraptor lived during the Cretaceous period.

In 1971, a fossil of *Velociraptor* and *Protoceratops* (pro-toe-SEH-rah-tops) locked in combat was found. *Protoceratops* was biting at the arm of the deadly predator, while *Velociraptor* attacked with its claws.

Protoceratops

Velociraptor

Giant southern reptile

Giganotosaurus (jee-gah-NOH-toh-SORE-us) was BIG! This massive meat eater lived 30 million years before *T. rex* came along, and was taller and heavier than its more famous cousin. Its teeth were as long as 8 inches (20 cm)—bigger than an adult's hand.

At 41 feet (12.5 m) long, *Giganotosaurus* was about the size of a bus. But its brain was only about the size of a banana!

Giganotosaurus means "giant southern lizard."

Fast Facts

When: Early Cretaceous period

Food: Other animals

Size: 41 ft (12.5 m) long

You!

Weight: 4.4 tons (4,000 kg)

How it moved: On two legs

Found in: Argentina, South America

A complete fossil of this dinosaur has never been found. But scientists think *Giganotosaurus* ate large plant-eating dinosaurs, such as *Argentinosaurus*.

Giganotosaurus' sharp teeth had saw-like edges.

Argentinosaurus

Nest builder

Oviraptor (OH-vee-RAP-tor) was a birdlike dinosaur covered with feathers. Its toothless beak and curved jaws crushed its food. It had a small crest like a horn on its snout. The crest may have been used for mating displays.

Oviraptor was probably an omnivore. It used its tough beak to crush food such as small lizards, fruit, and shellfish.

Oviraptor means "egg thief."

Oviraptor laid its eggs in nests. It sat on the eggs to keep them warm—just like a bird.

Fast Facts

When: Late Cretaceous period

Food: Meat, eggs, insects, shellfish, and plants

Size: 6.5 ft (2 m) long

You!

Weight: 44-66 lb (20-30 kg)

How it moved: On two legs

Found in: Mongolia, Asia

When the fossilized bones of *Oviraptor* were found in the nest of *Protoceratops*, scientists thought that *Oviraptor* was an egg thief. Now, they think the nest belonged to *Oviraptor*, and it was actually looking after its own eggs!

Protoceratops

Oviraptor was about the size of an emu.

Features of hunters

Meat eaters came in many shapes and sizes. However, they all had some things in common—the features that made them dangerous hunters.

Meat-eating dinosaurs had a powerful sense of smell and good eyesight.

They stood on their toes, and their strong legs helped them to catch prey quickly.

Super senses

Legs for running

Carcharodontosaurus
(CAR-kah-roh-don-toh-SORE-us)

Dilophosaurus
(dih-LOW-foh-SORE-us)

The skin or feathers of some hunters were patterned to help them blend into the background. This would have helped these mighty meat eaters to get close to their prey.

Meat-eating dinosaurs were smarter than plant eaters. They used their intelligence to hunt down other animals.

Brain power

Camouflage

Tarbosaurus
(TAR-bow-SORE-us)

Chindesaurus
(CHIN-dee-SORE-us)

T e terrible claw

Deinonychus (die-NOH-nih-kus) was a light and fast-moving dinosaur. It had a hunting claw on each foot. This meat eater was one of the smartest dinosaurs around—which made it a deadly predator!

Deinonychus was about 11 feet (3.4 m) long—that's twice as big as *Velociraptor*. It hunted in packs. It could use its huge claw to kick and tear its prey apart.

Deinonychus's hunting claw was 4.7 inches (12 cm) long!

Fast Facts

When: Early Cretaceous period

Food: Plant-eating dinosaurs

Size: 10 ft (3 m) long

You!

Weight: 165 lb (75 kg)

How it moved: On two legs

Found in: United States

This dinosaur may have been covered in feathers to keep it warm. The feathers also may have been used for mating displays!

Deinonychus means

"terrible claw."

Tyrant lizard

Tyrannosaurus rex is the most famous meat-eating dinosaur. With an excellent sense of smell and a fierce appetite, it may not have been the largest but it was the deadliest beast around.

T. rex's key feature was its huge head and powerful jaws filled with sharp teeth. Its bite could break bones so it could attack and eat most other dinosaurs. It would even fight rival tyrannosaurs for the chance of a bite to eat.

Its jaws could tear off 500 pounds (230 kg) of flesh at a time!

Tyrannosaurus rex means **"tyrant lizard king."**

T. rex had a high IQ, meaning it could plan its attacks on unsuspecting prey.

Fast Facts

When: Late Cretaceous period

Food: Other dinosaurs

Size: 39 ft (12 m) long

←You!

Weight: 7.7 tons (7,000 kg)

How it moved: On two legs

Found in: Canada and United States

Meat eaters around the world

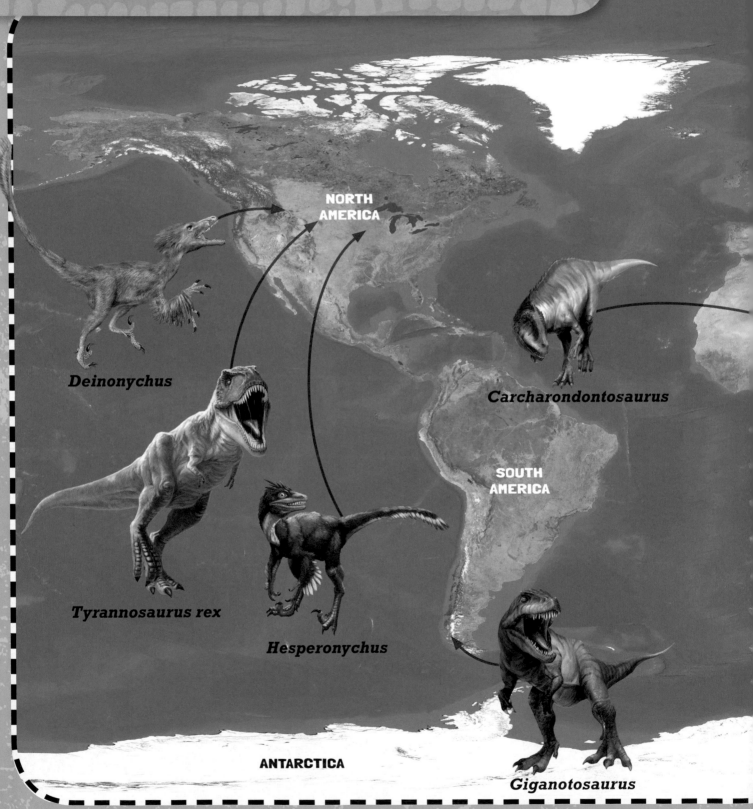

NORTH AMERICA

Deinonychus

Carcharondontosaurus

SOUTH AMERICA

Tyrannosaurus rex

Hesperonychus

ANTARCTICA

Giganotosaurus

The meat eaters featured in this book lived all over the world. Can you see one that would have existed near you?

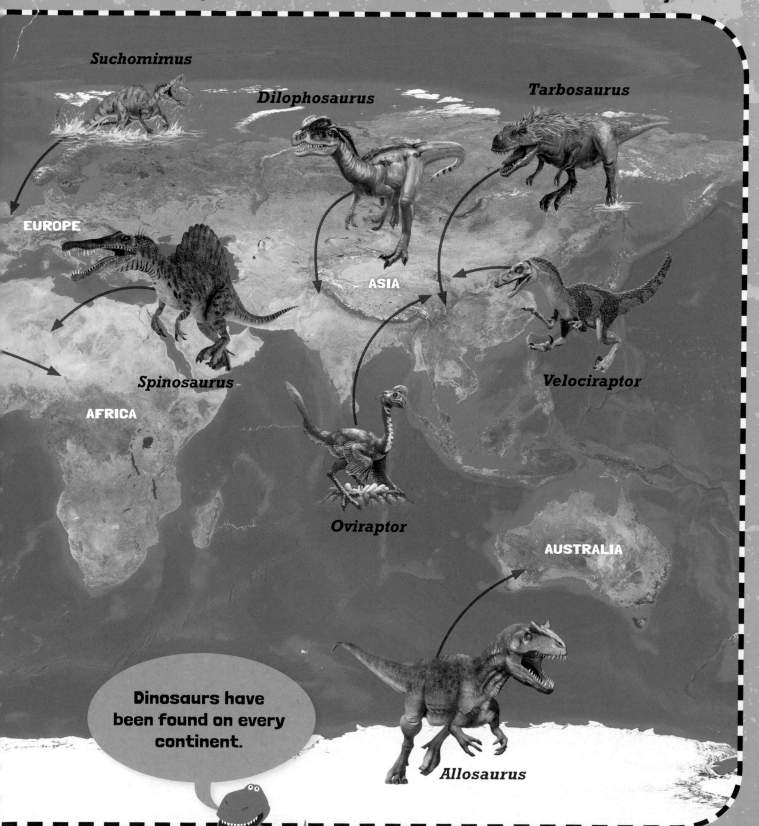

Suchomimus

Dilophosaurus

Tarbosaurus

EUROPE

Spinosaurus

ASIA

Velociraptor

AFRICA

Oviraptor

AUSTRALIA

Dinosaurs have been found on every continent.

Allosaurus

Glossary

adapt Change to new conditions.

appetite A desire to eat food.

camouflage The appearance of an animal, which helps it to blend in with its surroundings.

carnivore An animal that feeds on other animals.

crest A comb, tuft of feathers, fur or skin on the head of an animal.

Cretaceous period A period in Earth's history, between 144 and 65 million years ago.

enemy A dinosaur who is opposed to another dinosaur.

extinct No longer living.

fierce Violent, aggressive, or ferocious.

fossil The remains or imprint of an animal or plant, preserved for millions of years, now turned to stone.

frill A fringe of feathers or hair.

glide Move smoothly and continuously.

hunter An animal that searches and kills its prey.

jagged Rough, sharp edges.

Jurassic period A time in Earth's history, between 206 and 144 million years ago.

mate The partner of an animal.

pack A group of animals living together.

predator An animal that eats other animals.

prey An animal that is eaten by other animals.

saliva The watery liquid produced in the mouth to help chewing and swallowing.

sauropods Large, plant-eating dinosaurs with long necks and tails.

scavenger An animal that searches for and collects food.

serrated Having a jagged edge like a saw.

territory An area of land that an animal lives within and defends.

theropods A group of meat-eating dinosaurs.

Triassic period A period in Earth's history, between 248 and 206 million years ago.

Further information

Further reading

Beautiful Beasts, A Collection of Creatures Past and Present
by Camilla De La Baedoyaere (Sterling Children's Books, 2015)

The Dinosaur Hunter's Handbook
by Scott Forbes (Carlton Kids, 2015)

Dinosaurs: A Children's Encyclopedia
by editors of DK (Dorling Kindersley, 2011)

National Geographic Kids: The Ultimate Dinopedia
by Don Lessem (National Geographic Society, 2010)

Prehistoric Safari: Giant Dinosaurs
by Liz Miles (Franklin Watts, 2012)

The Usborne World Atlas of Dinosaurs
by Susanna Davidson (Usborne Publishing, 2013)

Websites

For web resources related to the subject of this book, go to:
www.windmillbooks.com/weblinks and select this book's title.

Index